To David, whose bookshelves introduced me
to the rest of the universe through Asimov,
Bradbury and Clarke, and who bought me *that*
Bowie record. – GA

For Rusty (the first dingo in space). – CN

BIG PICTURE PRESS

First published in the UK in 2019 by Big Picture Press,
an imprint of Bonnier Books UK,
The Plaza, 535 King's Road, London, SW10 0SZ
www.templarco.co.uk/big-picture-press
www.bonnierbooks.co.uk

1 3 5 7 9 10 8 6 4 2

ISBN 978-1-78741-354-2

This book was typeset in Burford Base and Rustic, Futura and Duality
The illustrations were created using a combination of traditional and digital techniques.

Edited by Katie Haworth
Designed by Nathalie Eyraud
Production Controller: Nick Read
Printed in China

Balloon to the Moon

Gill Arbuthnott • Christopher Nielsen

BPP

TIMELINE

15th–16th centuries: Leonardo da Vinci draws designs for flying machines

15th–16th centuries: Galileo Galilei discovers how to predict the paths of projectiles

17th century: Sir Isaac Newton publishes his Laws of Gravity (1666) and Laws of Motion (1686)

1232: Chinese use gunpowder-powered rockets as weapons

1783: The Montgolfier brothers demonstrate their invention, the hot air balloon

1877: Internal combustion engine invented

1891: Otto Lilienthal builds and flies his first glider

1903: The Wright brothers make the first powered, controlled aircraft flight

5th century BC: Kites invented in China

1926: Robert H Goddard launches the first liquid-powered rocket

1942: Wernher von Braun develops the V-2 missile

1947: Chuck Yeager breaks the sound barrier in the Bell X-1

1957: The Soviet Union launches Sputnik 1, the first satellite, into orbit

1957: Laika the dog becomes the first living creature to orbit Earth

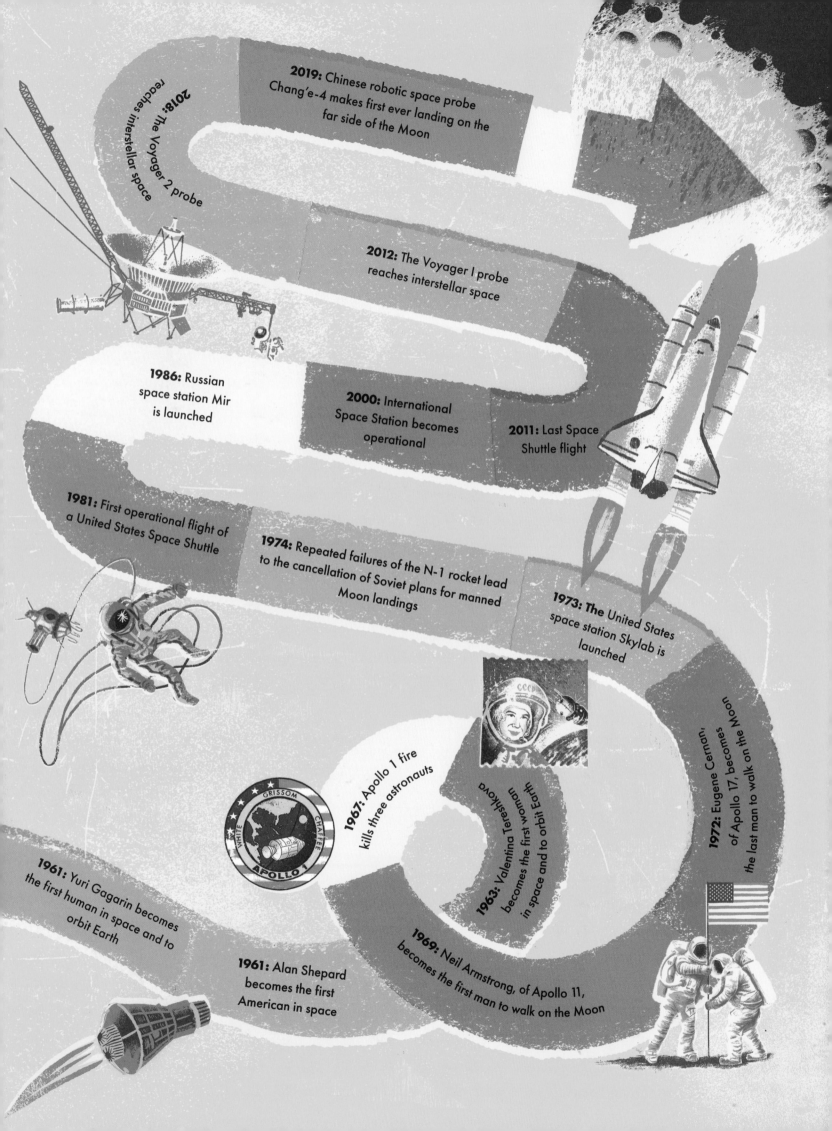

2019: Chinese robotic space probe Chang'e-4 makes first ever landing on the far side of the Moon

2018: The Voyager 2 probe reaches interstellar space

2012: The Voyager I probe reaches interstellar space

1986: Russian space station Mir is launched

2000: International Space Station becomes operational

2011: Last Space Shuttle flight

1981: First operational flight of a United States Space Shuttle

1974: Repeated failures of the N-1 rocket lead to the cancellation of Soviet plans for manned Moon landings

1973: The United States space station Skylab is launched

1967: Apollo 1 fire kills three astronauts

1963: Valentina Tereshkova becomes the first woman in space and to orbit Earth

1972: Eugene Cernan, of Apollo 17, becomes the last man to walk on the Moon

1961: Yuri Gagarin becomes the first human in space and to orbit Earth

1969: Neil Armstrong, of Apollo 11, becomes the first man to walk on the Moon

1961: Alan Shepard becomes the first American in space

FROM THE AUTHOR

It was July, 1969. Rock star David Bowie's song, 'Space Oddity' had just been released, and a few months previously the film *2001: A Space Odyssey* had made people look up at the stars and wonder . . .

At home, I watched a new TV show, *Star Trek*, on our small black-and-white television and marvelled at the futuristic detail. (Automatic doors! Hand-held communication devices!) As the Moon landing approached, my schoolfriends and I speculated about what the astronauts might find there: we were hopeful (and slightly worried) that there would be aliens. Science fiction was everywhere, but science fact was about to surpass it all.

My father had become more and more fascinated by the United States space programme as the 1960s progressed, and his interest had rubbed off on me, so on the night of 20 July, 1969, long after my normal bedtime, we sat riveted to the coverage of the Apollo 11 mission. Eventually, despite my protests, I was packed off to bed with the promise that I would be woken when the moment came for Neil Armstrong to step onto the surface of the Moon.

At 3.56 AM, breath held, we watched the grainy pictures of that historic step and the possibilities for the future seemed limitless. The entire universe was out there, just waiting for us.

I have never lost my fascination with space exploration, (though I have had to accept I will probably never be an astronaut), so the chance to tell the story of how humans reached the Moon was irresistible, especially once I discovered that it really began in France in 1783 with a sheep, a chicken, a duck – and a balloon . . .

Gill Arbuthnott

COUNTDOWN

In 1782, French paper manufacturers, Joseph-Michel and Jacques-Étienne Montgolfier, made a fascinating discovery. They realised that the hot air from a small fire could make a bag of cloth or paper rise into the air. They began to dream of balloons that could carry people into the sky.

The brothers gave a successful public demonstration in a large, unmanned balloon in June 1783, flying 300 metres. But how could they make sure that humans would survive in the sky?

The French King, Louis XVI, suggested experimenting with criminals, but the Montgolfiers decided to use animals instead and launched a balloon carrying a sheep, a duck and a chicken. They thought the sheep would be affected in the same way as a human; that the duck should be unharmed, as ducks fly at high altitudes; and that the chicken's reaction to balloon flight might provide interesting information, as chickens don't usually get far off the ground.

The animals returned, baffled but unharmed, from a 3 kilometre flight in front of Louis XVI and Queen Marie-Antoinette at the palace of Versailles, near Paris, on 19 September, 1783. Now, it was time for the first human aeronaut to lift off . . .

FIRST FLIGHT

Many of us have dreams where we can fly. We soar and hover like birds, and then we wake up — safely on the ground. When the Montgolfier brothers launched their first balloons, the idea of human flight was already ancient. For centuries people had risked their lives trying to take to the skies — some with more success than others.

ANCIENT GREECE

1. The idea of human flight even appears in ancient Greek mythology. According to legend, **Daedalus** was an inventor who made wax and feather wings for himself and his son, **Icarus**. He warned Icarus not to fly too high, or the heat of the sun would melt the wax. Icarus ignored the advice and fell to his death.

THE 5TH CENTURY BC

2. Kites were invented and flown in China from the 5th century BC. They were originally used for military purposes such as signalling, and some were supposedly large enough to lift people in what may be the first recorded example of human flight. There are reports that archers were lifted on kites to shoot at enemy soldiers. Enforced flights on kites also provided an unusual form of punishment.

THE 11TH CENTURY

3. Eilmer of Malmesbury was an 11th-century monk who made wings and launched himself from the tower of Malmesbury Abbey in Wiltshire, England. He apparently glided 200 metres before crash-landing and breaking both legs.

THE 19TH CENTURY

5. Jules Henri Giffard built and flew a steam-powered airship in 1852. This was the first powered flight. Giffard travelled 27 kilometres.

6. Otto Lilienthal, the 'Glider King' built and flew his first glider in 1891. He made over 2,000 flights in his gliders, and flew further and for longer than anyone had before. He was the first person to realise that a curved wing surface would provide more lift than a flat one – a discovery still used in modern planes.

THE 15TH–16TH CENTURIES

4. Leonardo da Vinci, the famous Renaissance artist and inventor, studied birds and how they flew. He designed many flying machines including gliders and parachutes. The best known is the ornithopter – a machine meant to be operated by a man flapping artificial wings. Unfortunately, there is no evidence that he ever built it.

6. 1862 Aeronauts **Henry Coxwell** and **James Glaisher** took off from Wolverhampton, England, intending to study the Earth's upper atmosphere. They estimated that they climbed to 11,000 metres. They suffered frostbite and oxygen deprivation, but landed safely.

8. 2005 **Vijaypat Singhania** piloted his hot air balloon *Envelope* to a world-record 21,290 metres in 2005, taking off from Mumbai, India, and landing safely almost five hours later.

7. 1999 The *Breitling Orbiter 3* became the first balloon to fly non-stop around the world, taking 19 days, 21 hours and 55 minutes. It was piloted by **Bertrand Piccard** and **Brian Jones**. The balloon reached an altitude of 11,000 metres and a speed of almost 300 kmh.

5. 1852–1937 Airships were huge bags of lighter-than-air gas, powered by an engine and propeller. Giffard's 1852 steam-powered airship (page 15) was followed by an electrically powered one in 1883, and in 1888 by the first with an internal combustion engine. By the 1920s airships were carrying passengers. On 6 May, 1937, the **Hindenburg**, a huge 244 metre long airship of a type known as a Zeppelin, burst into flames and crashed in New Jersey in the United States, killing 35 people. The world lost confidence in airships, but by then the age of the aeroplane had already begun.

BALLOON CRAZY

After the Montgolfier brothers conquered the air, people went balloon crazy. From the late 18th century, competitive balloonists set and broke records for speed, altitude and distance. In 1900, a new type of aircraft was also designed: the Zeppelin. These enormous airships were filled with lighter-than-air gases, either highly inflammable hydrogen or the much safer, non-inflammable helium.

4. 1798 The first woman to fly solo was **Jeanne-Geneviéve Labrosse**. Her husband's niece, **Élisa Garnerin**, was the first woman to parachute, a year later.

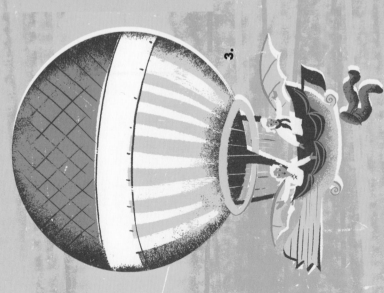

1.

1. 1783 The first manned, untethered flight was made by inventor **Pilâtre de Rozier** and the **Marquis d'Arlandes**, who travelled 8 kilometres in a Montgolfier balloon.

4.

3. 1785 The first crossing of the English Channel by air was made by Frenchman **Jean-Pierre Blanchard** and American **John Jeffries**. The two had to throw almost everything – including Blanchard's trousers – out of their balloon to stay airborne long enough to cross the channel.

2.

2. 1784 Nineteen-year-old **Elisabeth Thible**, an opera singer, became the first woman to take a trip in an untethered balloon, fetchingly dressed as the Roman goddess, Minerva.

3.

9

The First Aircraft

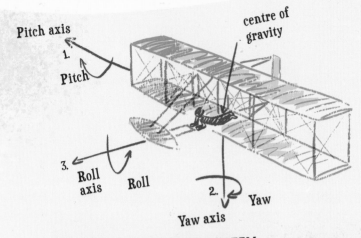

THE THREE-AXIS CONTROL SYSTEM:
1. Pitch axis – the nose of the aircraft can move up or down
2. Yaw axis – the nose of the aircraft can move from side to side
3. Roll axis – the wing tips can move up or down

Kites, balloons and gliders were all very well, but if humans were going to fly properly, they needed more reliable and controllable aircraft in which to do so, which meant powered heavier-than-air craft.

Kites and balloons were heavier than air of course, but they were at the mercy of the wind and couldn't be steered independently of it. In the 19th century, inventors like **Otto Lilienthal** (page 15) made great progress in understanding the principles of flight, but powered flight was still a dream.

Samuel Langley built a steam-powered model aircraft in the late 19th century, which flew successfully, but a steam engine powerful enough for a human-carrying plane was much too heavy to get off the ground. Meanwhile, the petrol-driven internal combustion engine, invented in 1877 and used in cars, was still in its infancy. And then one day in 1878, Milton Wright, a clergyman from Indiana in the United States, brought a toy 'helicopter' home to his sons **Wilbur and Orville Wright**.

From that day, the Wright brothers became obsessed with flying machines. At first they built gliders, but unlike other 'birdmen' they realised that birds change the angle of their wings to control their flight. From this they developed the three-axis control system – a revolutionary invention that is still used in aircraft.

THE FLYING WRIGHTS

Look! They twist their wings!

Let me make a sketch.

Orville and Wilber Wright wanted to build a flying machine. They studied nature . . .

. . . and between **1900** and **1902** they trialled a series of kites and man-carrying gliders to test their designs.

Next time you can be on board!

It works!

Now we just need an engine.

On 14 December, 1903, at Kill Devil Hills, Kitty Hawk, North Carolina, the Wright brother's aeroplane — complete with the first light aluminium engine — took off.

Wish me luck!

BUT THEN...

Orville and Wilber were undeterred. Three days later on 17 December, 1903 . . .

. . . they made their first flight. It lasted just 12 seconds and they travelled 37 metres.

The Wright brothers had made history.

They had achieved the first manned, powered, sustained and controlled flight.

EARLY AVIATORS

The Wright brothers had proved that controlled, powered flight was possible, and suddenly everyone wanted to fly. The first half of the 20th century saw records for speed and distance set and broken almost monthly. The men and women who were the pioneers of aviation became international celebrities.

LOUIS BLÉRIOT

LIVED: 1872–1936
FROM: CAMBRAI, FRANCE
PLANE FLOWN: BLÉRIOT TYPE XI MONOPLANE

In 1909, Blériot was the first person to cross the English Channel in a plane. He was also a successful aircraft designer and manufacturer *and* invented the first practical car headlamp.

JOHN ALCOCK AND ARTHUR BROWN

LIVED: 1892–1919 (ALCOCK); 1886–1948 (BROWN)
FROM: MANCHESTER, ENGLAND (ALCOCK); GLASGOW, SCOTLAND (BROWN)
PLANE FLOWN: VICKERS VIMY

Alcock and Brown made the first non-stop flight across the Atlantic Ocean in June 1919, from Newfoundland, Canada, to Ireland. Alcock was a pilot in the First World War and died in a flying accident in France in 1919. Brown joined the Royal Flying Corps and survived the war despite being shot down twice.

AMELIA EARHART 'QUEEN OF THE AIR'

LIVED: 1897–1937
FROM: KANSAS, UNITED STATES
PLANE FLOWN: MANY MODELS INCLUDING THE LOCKHEED VEGA 5B AND LOCKHEED ELECTRA 10E

In 1932, Earhart became the first woman to fly solo across the Atlantic Ocean. In 1937 she set off to fly around the world, but disappeared without trace while flying over the Pacific Ocean. Her fate remains a mystery.

BESSIE COLEMAN 'QUEEN BESS'

LIVED: 1892–1926
FROM: TEXAS, UNITED STATES
PLANE FLOWN: JN-4 'JENNY' BIPLANE

Coleman was the first African-American woman and the first woman of Native American descent to gain a pilot's licence. She wasn't allowed to study aviation in the United States in the 1920s because she was black, so she got her pilot's licence in France. She returned to the United States and became a stunt flyer, but died in 1926 when her mechanic crashed their plane.

NOTABLE AIRCRAFT

After the Wright brothers made the first controlled flight of a heavier-than-air craft, the age of aviation began. The first decades of the 20th century brought rapid advances in aircraft design. New technologies like rocket engines and supersonic flight would prove vital in the development of spacecraft.

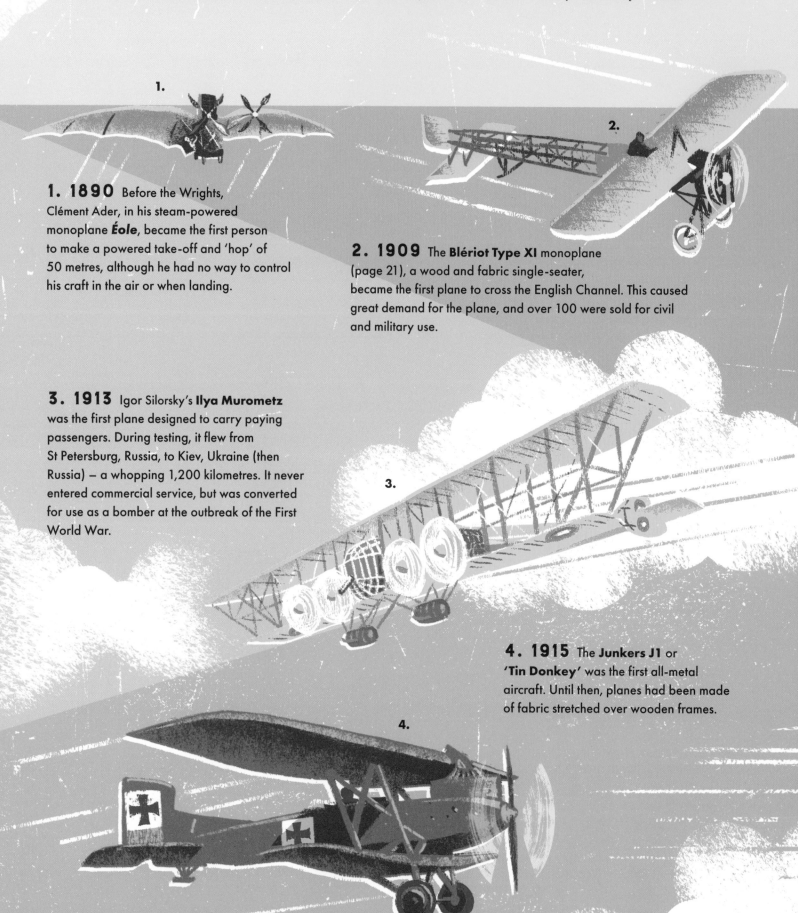

1. 1890 Before the Wrights, Clément Ader, in his steam-powered monoplane *Éole*, became the first person to make a powered take-off and 'hop' of 50 metres, although he had no way to control his craft in the air or when landing.

2. 1909 The **Blériot Type XI** monoplane (page 21), a wood and fabric single-seater, became the first plane to cross the English Channel. This caused great demand for the plane, and over 100 were sold for civil and military use.

3. 1913 Igor Silorsky's **Ilya Murometz** was the first plane designed to carry paying passengers. During testing, it flew from St Petersburg, Russia, to Kiev, Ukraine (then Russia) – a whopping 1,200 kilometres. It never entered commercial service, but was converted for use as a bomber at the outbreak of the First World War.

4. 1915 The **Junkers J1** or **'Tin Donkey'** was the first all-metal aircraft. Until then, planes had been made of fabric stretched over wooden frames.

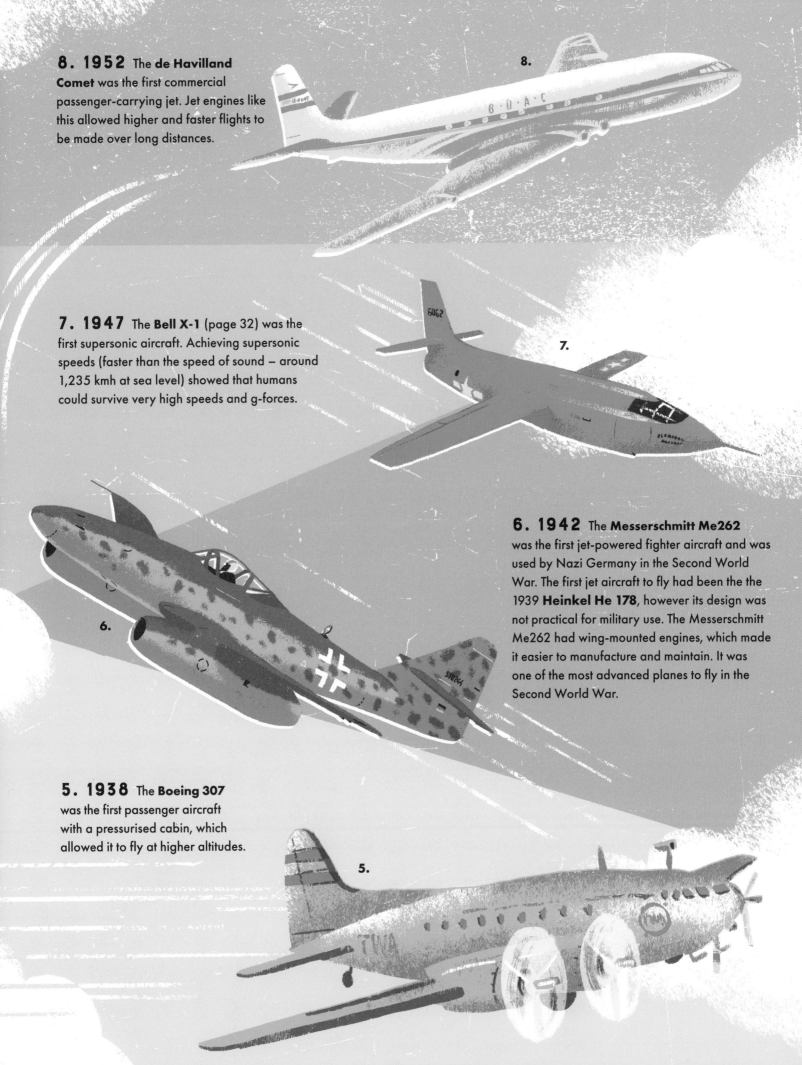

8. 1952 The **de Havilland Comet** was the first commercial passenger-carrying jet. Jet engines like this allowed higher and faster flights to be made over long distances.

8.

7. 1947 The **Bell X-1** (page 32) was the first supersonic aircraft. Achieving supersonic speeds (faster than the speed of sound – around 1,235 kmh at sea level) showed that humans could survive very high speeds and g-forces.

7.

6. 1942 The **Messerschmitt Me262** was the first jet-powered fighter aircraft and was used by Nazi Germany in the Second World War. The first jet aircraft to fly had been the the 1939 **Heinkel He 178**, however its design was not practical for military use. The Messerschmitt Me262 had wing-mounted engines, which made it easier to manufacture and maintain. It was one of the most advanced planes to fly in the Second World War.

6.

5. 1938 The **Boeing 307** was the first passenger aircraft with a pressurised cabin, which allowed it to fly at higher altitudes.

5.

Once they had taken to the skies, people began to wonder just how far they could go. Could humans reach space?

There had been huge technological advances in flight, but it was clear that aeroplanes wouldn't do the job outside Earth's atmosphere; that's because there's no air in space to provide lift for an aircraft's wings.

Rocket engines, however, don't need air: instead they work by pushing hot gas from the end of the rocket at high speed. Although they were originally developed as formidable flying weapons, scientists began to see other potential uses for rockets — could they carry passengers into space and bring them safely back?

In fact, science fiction had been exploring this idea for centuries.

In 1657, French author **Cyrano de Bergerac** may have been the first person to suggest reaching the Moon in a rocket, but the idea really fired the public's imagination with the publication of **Jules Verne's** *From the Earth to the Moon* in 1865. His 'rocket', was like a giant bullet which would be fired from an enormous gun. Verne actually tried to work out how large and powerful this gun would have to be, and was surprisingly accurate. However, in real life the rocket would have become so hot that it would have melted.

ROCKET SCIENCE

People started to make machines powered by hot gases thousands of years ago. Later, scientists like Galileo Galilei and Sir Isaac Newton experimented with the laws of physics and developed theories that would be vital for rocket technology.

HERO OF ALEXANDRIA

(1st century AD) was a Greek philosopher. He built Hero's Engine, the first recorded steam engine. It worked on the action-reaction principle which Isaac Newton later identified.

GALILEO GALILEI

(1564–1642) showed that objects fall at the same rate, regardless of their weight. He discovered that the path followed by projectiles – such as rockets – was determined by their velocity (speed) and the effect of gravity, and so could be predicted. He is best remembered as the first person to properly study the night sky with a telescope.

SIR ISAAC NEWTON (1642–1727) published

his Laws of Gravity in 1666 and his Laws of Motion in 1686.

NEWTON'S LAWS OF MOTION

 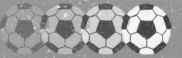

A. **B.**

1. The Law of Inertia: An object stays at rest if it is already at rest, or keeps moving in a straight line if it is already moving, unless a force acts on it.

A. No force. Ball does not move. **B.** Ball moves on frictionless surface (friction is a force). It won't stop until it meets an outside force.

A. **B.**

2. The Law of Force: Force (F) = mass (m) x acceleration (a). The acceleration (change of motion) of an object depends on its mass, and how much force you apply to it.

If you hit an old leather softball (**A.**) and a modern plastic one (**B.**) with equal force, the plastic one will travel faster and further, because it is lighter.

3. Every action produces an **equal and opposite reaction**. If the skateboarders push against each other, their skateboards will move in the opposite direction.

The theories of Galileo and Newton were the basis for the subsequent development of rockets and their use in space exploration.

ROCKETS TAKE OFF

The word 'rocket' didn't exist when the first rockets were used, but these weapons were the forerunners of the rockets that would take humans to the Moon. Space exploration owes a lot to technologies developed to fight wars.

1. 1232 The first true rockets were Chinese fire arrows – gunpowder-fuelled rockets used as weapons in battle between the Chinese and Mongolian armies in 1232.

2. 17TH–19TH CENTURIES In 1650
Casimir Siemienowicz, a Polish-Lithuanian rocket expert, wrote an important book on artillery rockets. This led to a renewed interest in rockets as weapons and Congreve Rockets were used in the Napoleonic Wars (1799–1815).

3. LATE 19TH CENTURY
Russian maths teacher, **Konstantin Tsiolkovsky**, realised that rockets provided a way – in theory at least – for people to reach space. He began to write about spacecraft design in 1895. Tsiolkovsky worked out that liquid fuel (which can achieve a more sustained thrust than gunpowder) and a sealed cabin with an oxygen supply would be needed. He also proposed the use of satellites.

4. 1926 American physicist **Robert H Goddard**, aka the 'Moon Rocket Man', was the first to test his theories about rocket flight by experimenting, and, in 1926, launched the first liquid-powered rocket in history from his Aunt Effie's cabbage patch in Massachusetts in the United States.

5. 1942 **Wernher von Braun** developed the V-2 rocket missile for Nazi Germany during the Second World War. This terrifying weapon, first launched in 1942, was the beginning of human-made technology that could reach space.

HOW DO ROCKETS WORK?

Rockets obey Newton's third Law of Motion: "Every action produces an equal and opposite reaction" (page 26). In jet aircraft, the engine power pushes against air so the plane moves. In space there is no air, so how do rockets work? Rocket engines burn fuel to produce hot exhaust gas. This is forced from the back of the rocket at high pressure so it pushes the rocket forwards.

The payload: This is what the rocket is carrying. It may be a manned capsule or a satellite.

The shape of the rocket: This minimises air resistance – drag – which acts to pull the rocket down during lift off. Long, smooth, pointed shapes have low drag: rockets, bullet trains and sharks are all examples.

Fuel tank: Most of a rocket is made up of tanks for fuel and oxygen storage. Some use solid fuel, but many use liquid fuel, usually hydrogen.

Oxidiser tank: To burn anything – including rocket fuel – you need oxygen and there's none in space. Rockets have to carry oxygen too.

Fuel pump

Oxygen pump

Combustion chamber: The fuel and oxygen are mixed and burn here.

Exhaust: Hot exhaust gas blasts out of the back of the rocket. This pushes against the rocket and the rocket pushes against the gas. This is what makes a rocket accelerate.

THE FIRST SATELLITES

Sergei Korolev was one of the most influential inventors in the history of space flight. Because of the secrecy that sourrounded the Soviet space programme, he was only known as 'The Chief Designer' until his death in 1966. After the Second World War he had studied the German V-2 rocket and modified it to dramatically increase its range from 320 kilometres to 685 kilometres. His invention, the R-7 ballistic missile, had the rocket power needed to lauch the first satellite into orbit on 4 October, 1957.

This satellite was **Sputnik-1**, a 58-centimetre ball, weighing 84 kilograms and with 4 radio antennae. Until its batteries ran out after 21 days, it sent radio signals back to Earth. It was gradually pulled in by the Earth's magnetic field, and burned up in the atmosphere on 4 January, 1958.

*Humans had been looking at the stars for thousands of years,
but now, with developments in rocket design and power, it began to look
as though they really might be able to travel to space.*

This led to a new question – what effect would the g-forces caused by acceleration at
lift-off and travelling at such enormous speeds have on the human body? And would
people be able to carry out tasks if they were weightless in space? Surprisingly, some of
the most important answers came, not from experiments with rockets, but from test pilots
flying the world's most powerful – and dangerous – planes.

What are g-forces?

If you stand still on Earth, you experience Earth gravity – 1g. The force exerted on an
object in relation to the size of Earth's gravity is g-force.

If you go up in a high-speed lift, the lift exerts a bigger force on you than the Earth's gravity.
The faster your speed changes, the higher the force you experience and the easiest way to
express this is as a multiple of the pull of gravity, g. Astronauts don't usually experience a
force much more than 3g, but fighter pilots have to deal with forces of up to 9g.

SUPERSONIC MAN

It was 1947, and in the years since the first jet flight (page 23), jet aircraft had grown more powerful and could fly much faster. The speed of sound (1,235 kmh at sea level), which is called Mach 1, was within reach. But what would happen to an aircraft – and its pilot – if they did break the legendary sound barrier?
Captain Chuck Yeager was about to find out . . .

THE RACE FOR MACH 1

Although it wasn't the aim at the time, achieving this speed and knowing how it affected the body would be crucial in the development of rockets that could escape the pull of Earth's gravity.

As planes neared Mach 1, they became more unstable and harder to control. This had already caused the death of a number of test pilots, but there was still great competition to be the first pilot to reach Mach 1.

THE PILOT

Captain Chuck Yeager had already reached Mach .94 in the Bell X-1 aircraft he had named *Glamorous Glennis* after his wife. Now he was to attempt to break the sound barrier.

The night before the flight, Yeager broke two ribs after a horse kicked him. He persuaded a doctor to tape the injury – and not report it – but he couldn't use his right arm properly, and he needed it to fasten the cockpit door. He confessed to fellow pilot, Jack Ridley, who came up with a way for Yeager to close the door with a piece of broom handle.

TAKE-OFF

On 14 October, 1947, Yeager took off in the **Bell X-1**, *Glamorous Glennis*. He was ready to attempt what had never been done before.

FASTER THAN SOUND

Then the shaking stopped, the aircraft flew smoothly and the people on the ground heard the world's first **sonic boom**. Yeager had hit Mach 1.

SPEEDING UP

As Yeager's speed approached Mach 1, *Glamorous Glennis* began to shake, getting harder and harder to control.

WHAT IS A SONIC BOOM?

A sonic boom is caused by a plane travelling faster than the sound waves it creates. The waves are squashed together and trail behind it, like the 'wake' of waves behind a fast boat. When the sound waves reach you – after the plane has gone past – you hear a booming noise.

THE LEGACY

On 14 October, 2012, Yeager celebrated the 65th anniversary of breaking the sound barrier by doing it again at the age of 89, this time as a passenger in an F-15 jet.

ANIMALS IN SPACE

The first astronauts were animals. Humans would reach space in April, 1961, but many other creatures had already been there. Just as the Montgolfiers had used animals to study the effects of balloon flight, scientists were now using them to find out if living things could survive space flight, with its weightlessness and high g-forces. Animal test flights, like the ones described here, showed that life support systems worked and that humans could go into space and come back alive.

MEET SOME OF THE PIONEERING ASTROBEASTS!

TINY FRUIT FLIES were the first animals in space, launched from the United States on a V-2 rocket in 1947. They reached a height of 109 kilometres before parachuting (in a container, not on tiny individual parachutes!) safely back to Earth.

ALBERT II became the first monkey in space in 1948. Launched by the United States, he went 130 kilometres from Earth, but unfortunately he died when the rocket's parachute failed.

FÉLICETTE a black-and-white French moggy, was the only cat to take a space flight. In 1963, she returned safely from a flight that reached an altitude of 160 kilometres.

LAIKA was the most famous of the dogs that the Soviet Union (the 1922–1991 socialist union of states that included Russia and many surrounding countries) sent into space in the 1950s. She became the first living creature to orbit Earth in 1957, but died during the flight. In 1960, the dogs Belka and Strelka became the first animals to orbit Earth and come back alive.

HAM AND ENOS the astrochimps, flew as part of the American Mercury missions in 1961–1962. Unlike the other animals, who were simply passengers, they were trained to carry out basic tasks such as pulling a series of levers, and their performances on Earth and in space were compared.

Enos orbited Earth in 1961, in a rehearsal for John Glenn's historic flight (page 39), and died in 1962. Ham died in 1983 and is buried at the International Space Hall of Fame in New Mexico in the United States.

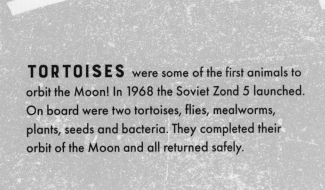

TORTOISES were some of the first animals to orbit the Moon! In 1968 the Soviet Zond 5 launched. On board were two tortoises, flies, mealworms, plants, seeds and bacteria. They completed their orbit of the Moon and all returned safely.

6

HUMANS in SPACE

Animal pioneers had provided a huge amount of valuable medical data, but there was only one way to really know how space travel would affect a human.

In March, 1961, Nikita Khrushchev, the leader of the Soviet Union announced, "The time is not far off when the first spaceship with a man on board will soar into space."

Astronauts had been the heroes and heroines of science fiction stories for years; now fiction was about to become fact. The risks in sending humans into space were enormous, and highly skilled, highly trained, hugely courageous volunteers were needed for this job.

To go to space, a human would have to be strapped into a rocket filled with explosive kerosene and liquid oxygen. It would accelerate to 40,000 kmh on the way up, and he or she would then have to trust that their space capsule's heat shield would cope with temperatures of up to 1,650°C as it re-entered Earth's atmosphere — and that the parachute would open on the way down . . .

What type of man or woman would be brave enough to volunteer?

EARLY SPACE EXPLORERS

The United States and the Soviet Union were each determined to be the first to put a human into space and, between 1959 and 1960, both countries began selecting who would go. In the Soviet Union these people were called Cosmonauts (from Greek words meaning 'universe sailor') and in the United States they were called astronauts (from Greek words meaning 'star sailor'). Both cosmonauts and astronauts were training for the same dangerous job.

COSMONAUTS

YURI GAGARIN was used to danger long before he stepped into a rocket; in 1941, when he was seven, the village of Klushino where he lived was occupied by the Nazis. In 1960 he was one of 20 pilots selected as possible cosmonauts because of his fitness, motivation and focus . . . and because his good looks made him perfect for Soviet propaganda.

On 12 April, 1961, he blasted off from Baikonur Cosmodrome in Kazakhstan and orbited the Earth once in the Vostok 1 capsule. The first manned space flight lasted 108 minutes. Gagarin returned to Earth an international celebrity. He died in 1968 on a routine test flight.

VALENTINA TERESHKOVA was born in 1937. She left school at 16, and learned to skydive at the air-sports club of the factory she worked at. After Gagarin's flight, she applied for the space programme, saying, "If women can be railroad workers in Russia, why can't they fly in space?" She was one of five women chosen from over 400 applicants.

On 16 June, 1963, she became the first woman to go into space, piloting **Vostok 6**, in which she orbited Earth 48 times. The flight lasted over 70 hours. Internationally famous since her pioneering space flight, she lit the Olympic cauldron at the Sochi Winter Olympics in 2014.

ASTRONAUTS

ALAN SHEPARD served with the United States Navy in the Second World War, and became a test pilot in 1950. After being selected as one of the 'Mercury 7' first astronauts by NASA (the National Aeronautics and Space Administration), he was chosen for the first manned American space flight, which took place on 5 May, 1961. This lasted 15.5 minutes and did not enter Earth orbit.

Although this first flight had been brief, it sparked the imagination of United States President, John F Kennedy, who, three weeks later, announced America's plan to put a man on the Moon before the end of the decade. Shepard later became the only one of the Mercury 7 to walk on the Moon.

VIRGIL 'GUS' GRISSOM became an air cadet during the Second World War and flew over 100 combat missions in the Korean War (1950–1953). After qualifying as a test pilot, he was selected to join the space programme. He was nearly disqualified when they found he suffered from hay fever – until someone pointed out that there was no pollen in space!

Grissom was chosen to be the second American in space for a short, also non-orbital, flight on 21 July, 1961. After splashdown, the hatch of his capsule blew off and the capsule began to sink. Grissom nearly drowned. He became the first man to go into space twice when he flew in the Gemini 3 mission in 1965. He was killed in the Apollo 1 disaster in 1967 (page 49).

JOHN GLENN was a United States Marine pilot in both the Second World War and the Korean War. After qualifying as a test pilot, he made the first supersonic transcontinental flight in 1957, flying 3,935 kilometres across the United States in 3 hours and 23 minutes.

On 20 February, 1962, he became the first American to orbit Earth, completing three orbits. A sensor indicated that his heat shield was faulty, which could have caused the craft to burn up on re-entry, but fortunately only the sensor was broken and he splashed down safely. In 1998, aged 77, he became the oldest person to go into space.

Are you under 180 centimetres tall?
Are you under 82 kilograms and in excellent physical condition?
Are you under 40 years old, and do you have a degree?
Are you a military test pilot, qualified to fly jets, and with
at least 1,500 hours of flying experience?
Oh – and are you a man?

These were the criteria NASA applied when considering who they should send to space. More than 500 qualified men were identified in January, 1959. Of these, 69 were selected for testing and after interviews, exams, running miles on treadmills, blowing up balloons until they were exhausted and having every inch of their bodies probed and tested, the **Mercury 7** were chosen and unveiled to the world in April, 1969.

These were the first American astronauts and they were trained for the Mercury missions. As well as **Alan Shepard**, **Virgil 'Gus' Grissom** and **John Glenn** (page 39), the Mercury 7 included: **Scott Carpenter**, **Gordon 'Gordo' Cooper**, **Walter 'Wally' Schirra** and **Donald 'Deke' Slayton**.

What exactly did they go through, as they prepared to survive in space? Would you cope with astronaut training?

WELCOME TO ASTRONAUT TRAINING!

Congratulations on passing our rigorous selection process. You have been chosen to be one of the Mercury 7. But this is only the beginning of your journey to space. Here's a guide to what to expect as we assess your chances of making it there and back in perfect health and without breaking our very expensive rocket.

PHYSICAL TESTS

We'll be measuring your endurance under conditions you might experience in space. How much noise and heat can you take? And how will you cope with almost 100 times more carbon dioxide than normal?

PSYCHOLOGICAL TESTS

We need to be sure you can cope with the mental pressures of space travel, so we'll carry out psychological tests. We'll simulate up to 12 things going wrong at once in your spacecraft. Will you panic?

SURVIVAL TRAINING

In case your capsule lands somewhere it wasn't meant to, we'll teach you to survive in the desert and jungle. Amongst other things, you'll learn how to make a tent from your parachute and how to kill and eat a snake.

WEIGHTLESS TRAINING

It is tricky to replicate weightlessness on Earth, but the best way is to make you swim underwater, weighted so you don't bob to the surface.

VOMIT COMET

We'll also send you up for flights on the Vomit Comet. That's a plane that climbs and drops repeatedly, like a rollercoaster, as it flies. This gives you 30–40 periods of weightlessness each lasting about 25 seconds. Why is it called the Vomit Comet? Don't worry, you'll find out.

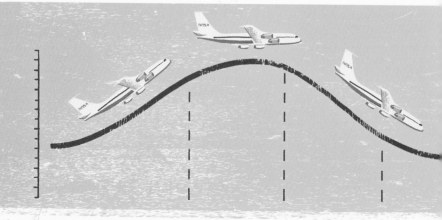

THE 'GIMBAL RIG'

You'll love this. We can spin you around in any direction in this machine, as though your capsule is out of control. You have the fun of trying to stabilise it again.

HIGH-G TRAINING

Welcome to the Centrifuge! We're going to spin you round in this machine very, very quickly, to subject you to the sort of g-forces you'll face on lift-off and re-entry.

FLIGHT SIMULATOR TRAINING

Get used to the simulator, because you are going to spend around 2,000 hours in it between now and lift-off, going over and over everything that could possibly happen during your flight.

YOUR SPACE SUIT

You'll be wearing a pressure suit during your flight, just in case the space capsule springs a leak. If that happens, the suit will squeeze your body tightly, and supply you with oxygen at the right pressure so that inside it you are still in Earth-like conditions and can breathe. Slip into it now so we can check it out!

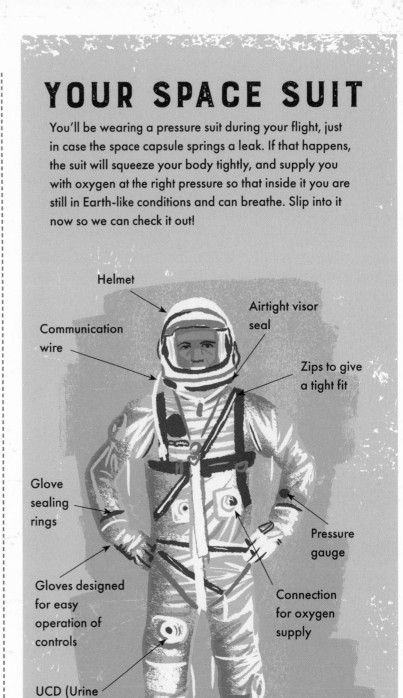

Helmet

Communication wire

Airtight visor seal

Zips to give a tight fit

Glove sealing rings

Gloves designed for easy operation of controls

Pressure gauge

Connection for oxygen supply

UCD (Urine collection device outlet)

Silver outer layer helps control temperature

Boots

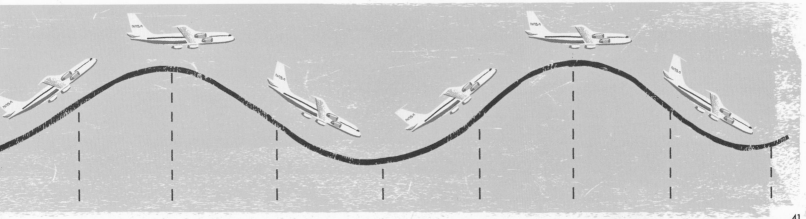

4

RACE to the MOON

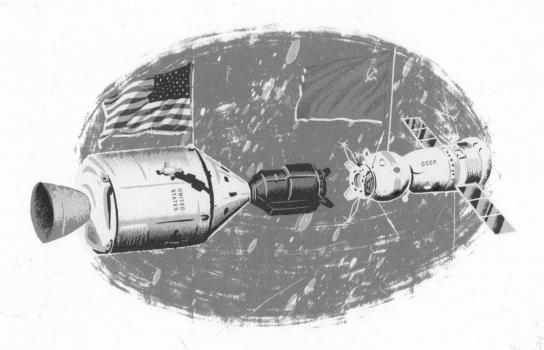

After joining forces to fight and defeat the Nazis in the Second World War, the world 'superpowers', the United States and the Soviet Union, grew deeply suspicious of each other.

An arms race developed as each side tried to come up with the most powerful weapons, including nuclear bombs and missiles. This period of hostility is known as the Cold War because, despite the development of weapons, the two sides never actually fought each other. Space Missions became another high-profile way for the rivals to show how powerful their technology had become.

Wernher von Braun (page 27), the leading scientist in the development of the V-2 rocket, and his team surrendered to the United States at the end of the Second World War. In 1959 they were joined in the United States by **Hermann Oberth** — von Braun's former mentor — and together they made huge contributions to the development of rockets.

On the Soviet side **Sergei Korolev**, 'The Chief Designer' (page 29), developed technology that initially helped the Soviet Union take the lead in what became known as the 'Space Race'.

The Space Race really began when both sides announced in 1955 that they intended to put satellites into orbit, and it ended in 1975 when the United States Apollo, and Soviet Soyuz crafts rendezvoused in space. Between those dates, both sides achieved many milestones in space exploration — and both had plans to land on the Moon . . .

THE SPACE RACE

After the successful launch of Sputnik 1, space flights came thick and fast, with records set and broken by both the United States and Soviet Union, as missions became longer and more complex.

SOVIET UNION

4 October: The first successful artificial satellite launch of Sputnik 1.

3 November: Sputnik 2 is launched carrying Laika the dog.

2 January: Luna 1 is the first craft launched to the Moon. It is the first man-made object to escape Earth's gravitational field.

12 September: Luna 2 becomes the first craft on the Moon after crash landing.

7 October: Luna 3 sends back the first pictures of the far side of the Moon.

April 12: Yuri Gagarin in Vostok 1 becomes the first human in space and the first to orbit Earth.

11 August: First simultaneous flight of two craft in space as Vostok 3 and 4 are both in Earth orbit at the same time.

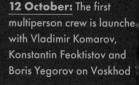

June 16: Valentina Tereshkova becomes the first woman in space.

12 October: The first multiperson crew is launched with Vladimir Komarov, Konstantin Feoktistov and Boris Yegorov on Voskhod

1957	1958	1959	1961	1962	1963	1964

6 December: Failed launch of the Vanguard Test Vehicle 3 (TV3) satellite.

31 January: First United States satellite, Explorer 1, is launched.

7 August: First photograph of Earth from space is sent back by Explorer 6.

5 May: Alan Shepard in Mercury spacecraft *Freedom 7* is the first American in space. President Kennedy vows to send men to the Moon by the end of the decade.

20 February: First American to orbit Earth is John Glenn in Mercury.

31 July: First close ups of Moon sent back by unmanned Ranger 7.

UNITED STATES

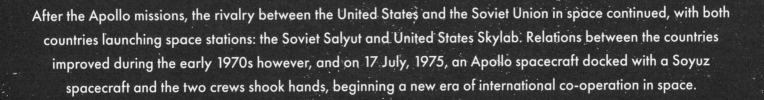

After the Apollo missions, the rivalry between the United States and the Soviet Union in space continued, with both countries launching space stations: the Soviet Salyut and United States Skylab. Relations between the countries improved during the early 1970s however, and on 17 July, 1975, an Apollo spacecraft docked with a Soyuz spacecraft and the two crews shook hands, beginning a new era of international co-operation in space.

14 January: Sergei Korolev, 'Chief Designer' dies. His death changes the focus of the Soviet space programme. The N-1 rocket's design is never finalised.

31 January: Luna 9 makes the first controlled Moon landing and sends pictures to Earth.

31 March: Luna 10 becomes the first spacecraft to orbit the Moon.

15 September: Zond 5 becomes the first unmanned craft to orbit the Moon and return to Earth.

Two further N-1 failures lead to the cancellation of the Soviet Union Moon-landing project.

18 March: Alexei Leonov makes the first spacewalk from Voskhod 2.

23 April: Vladimir Komarov is the first cosmonaut to die on a space mission. This was due to faults in his craft, Soyuz 1.

16 January: Soyuz 4 and 5 complete the first transfer of crew between spacecraft.

21 February, 3 July: Two N-1 rockets, meant to take the Soviet Union to the Moon, are destroyed in failed launches.

CCCP

| 1965 | 1966 | 1967 | 1968 | 1969 | 1971-1972 |

23 March: Gemini 3 takes two astronauts into space. The Gemini missions will help prepare astronauts and spacecraft for manned Moon landings.

3 June: The first American to spacewalk is Ed White from Gemini 4.

15 December: Gemini 6 and 7 make the first planned meeting of vehicles in space.

27 January: The first Apollo mission. Gus Grissom, Ed White and Roger Chaffee are killed in a fire during a preflight test.

March 16: Gemini 8 is the first vehicle to dock (connect to another vehicle) in space.

May 30: Surveyor 1 is the first American spaceship to land on the Moon.

October 11: Apollo 7, the first manned Apollo mission, orbits Earth for 11 days.

December 21: The Apollo 8 mission makes astronauts Frank Borman, James Lovell and William Anders the first humans to orbit the Moon.

20 July: Apollo 11. The first humans – Neil Armstrong and Buzz Aldrin – land on the Moon and return to Earth safely.

3

AMERICA heads for THE MOON

"Why, some say, the Moon? Why choose this as our goal? And they may well ask, why climb the highest mountain? . . . We choose to go to the Moon in this decade and do the other things, not because they are easy, but because they are hard . . ."

In September 1962, United States President John F Kennedy made a speech to persuade people that the Apollo programme would be worthwhile. The Mercury missions had sent astronauts into Earth orbit and returned them safely, but the longest flight had only lasted 34 hours. If the United States was to reach the Moon, crews would have to learn how to live and work in space for days at a time.

In 1965 and 1966, the thirteen Gemini missions demonstrated that space flights lasting many days were possible. The Gemini (meaning 'twins') capsules carried two astronauts who stayed in space for up to two weeks at a time.

The success of Project Gemini paved the way for the Apollo missions, the aims of which were to land astronauts on the Moon. On 21 February, 1967, **Gus Grissom**, **Ed White** and **Roger Chaffee** climbed into the Command Module of Apollo 1 to rehearse launch procedures. They were sealed in and surrounded by highly flammable 100 percent oxygen.

After five hours, a fire broke out, and within minutes all three men were dead. After this tragedy, manned flights were suspended while new safety features were introduced.

SATURN V

The Saturn V rocket was the vehicle that launched many of the Apollo missions into space. It had 13 successful flights between 1967 and 1973. The rocket's launch was divided into stages, with only the Command Module returning to Earth to be used again.

Escape Rocket: If a launch goes wrong, this fires to separate the Command Module from the rest of the rocket and propel it to safety.

Apollo Command Module, *Colombia*: The crew cabin in which the three astronauts travel to and from the Moon.

Service Module: Houses the engines, fuel, oxygen, and water for the mission. It separates from the Command Module just before re-entry.

Lunar Module, *the Eagle*: Separates from the Command Module in lunar orbit to allow two astronauts to land and take off from the Moon. This is a two-stage vehicle. The Descent stage remains on the Moon after the astronauts leave. The Ascent stage launches back into space and docks with the Command Module.

Third Stage S-IVB: This fires once to put the craft into Earth orbit, and again once there to break away from Earth orbit and send the craft to the Moon. It separates from the Command, Service and Lunar Modules and is then sent into orbit around the Sun or crashes into the Moon.

Liquid hydrogen fuel

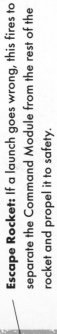

APOLLO SPACECRAFT

THE FIRST APOLLO MISSIONS

The Apollo 1 fire revealed that safety had been compromised in the rush to get the programme off the ground. Major changes were made to the spaceship's design, and the atmosphere inside was changed from 100 percent oxygen to a less flammable 60 percent oxygen, 40 percent nitrogen during ground tests – although it was still 100 percent oxygen in space. Spacesuits were now made with non-flammable material and the insulation of wiring was greatly improved, as was the ground crews' emergency training and equipment.

EARLY APOLLO FLIGHTS

Although manned flights were suspended for 20 months after the fire, unmanned flights resumed later in 1967. During this time, the new safety features were introduced.

AS 201, 202, 203

were unmanned test flights made before Apollo 1, to test fuel systems under weightless conditions, guidance and navigation and, crucially, whether a rocket could be restarted in Earth orbit to fire a craft towards the Moon.

Second Stage S-II: Contains liquid hydrogen fuel and oxygen. This fires for 6 minutes, taking the craft to an altitude of 175 kilometres, then separates and falls into the sea.

Liquid hydrogen fuel

Liquid oxygen

First Stage S-IC: This powers the lift-off.

Liquid oxygen

Kerosene fuel

Five engines fire to lift the rocket from the launch pad to an altitude of 68 kilometres. Once the fuel is exhausted, this stage falls into the sea.

93 metres

111 metres

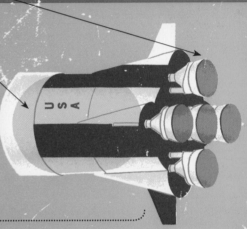

STAGES OF THE SATURN V ROCKET LAUNCH

APOLLO 4, 9 November, 1967: This was the first launch since Apollo 1 and the first test launch of a Saturn V rocket. It had been delayed to make changes to improve safety, following the Apollo 1 disaster. To NASA's relief, the flight went perfectly.

APOLLO 5, 22 January, 1968: This was the first time the Lunar Module, the part of the craft that would take astronauts down to the Moon's surface, had been taken into space. During this flight the systems which would allow it to land and take off again were tested.

APOLLO 6, 4 April, 1968: The final unmanned Apollo mission was meant to fire the third-stage rocket engines while in Earth orbit to send the spacecraft towards the Moon. Engine and fuel flow problems prevented this but, crucially, allowed them to be corrected before the first manned Apollo flight.

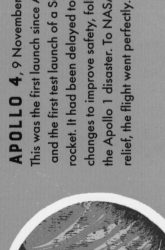

Once all safety improvements from the Apollo 1 enquiry had been tested on unmanned flights, the Apollo 7 mission – launched on 11 October, 1968 – put humans back into space.

To everyone's relief, the mission was a success. The astronauts spent 11 days in space, completing 163 orbits of Earth, testing new operating systems and spacesuits, and trying out the Block II Command Module for the first time.

The astronauts' fitness was tested on exercise bikes before and after the flight. The tests indicated that muscles could begin to waste in weightless conditions. Astronauts in space now exercise every day to prevent this.

Astronauts **Donn Eisele** and **Walter Schirra** developed colds during the mission. In micro-gravity, all the mucus got stuck inside their heads, leaving them very uncomfortable; the only way to clear it was to blow their noses very hard, which made their ear drums hurt. They refused to wear their helmets for re-entry, afraid that if they couldn't blow their noses, the pressure might make their eardrums burst!

Television footage of the astronauts floating weightlessly and eating 'space food' as well as front-page stories in many United States newspapers rekindled the public's fascination with the Apollo programme.

APOLLO 8 AND
THE FAR SIDE OF THE MOON

With all systems checked and ready to go, astronauts **Frank Borman**, **James Lovell** and
William Anders became the first to take the awesome step of leaving behind the relative safety of
Earth orbit and orbiting the Moon itself.

Apollo 8 launched on **21 December, 1968,** and arrived in lunar orbit three days later. On Christmas Eve, the astronauts made a live TV broadcast from lunar orbit, sending back pictures of the Earth and Moon and reading from the Bible. They ended the broadcast by saying, "Goodnight, Good Luck, a Merry Christmas and God bless you all – all of you on the good Earth." The broadcast was heard by almost 1 billion people in 64 countries.

THE FAR SIDE OF THE MOON

The far side of the Moon is the side that we do not see from Earth. The Moon takes the same time to rotate once as it takes to orbit our planet, so the same side always faces us. The first photographs of the far side were taken by the Soviet Luna 3 probe in 1959 and the crew of Apollo 8 were the first humans ever to see it for themselves. The surface of the far side is much rougher than the side you can see from Earth, with many craters, which makes it much harder to land spacecraft there.

EARTHRISE

On their fourth orbit of the Moon, the crew of Apollo 8 became the first people to see Earthrise. They rushed to take the first picture of it captured by humans in lunar orbit.

Look at that picture over there! Here's the Earth coming up. Wow, is that pretty!

Borman later said: "It was the most beautiful, heart-catching sight of my life, one that sent a torrent of nostalgia, of sheer homesickness, surging through me. It was the only thing in space that had any colour to it. Everything was either black or white. But not the Earth."

APOLLO 9 AND 10 – THE DRESS REHEARSALS

However many tests and simulations were run on the ground, they couldn't properly replicate what would have to happen for a successful Moon landing. Everything had to be tried out in space.

APOLLO 9

The primary mission of Apollo 9 was to fly the Lunar Module for the first time. It would have to work independently from the Command Module during a Moon landing.

Although he couldn't go far due to Space Adaptation Sickness (like sea sickness in space), **Russell Schweickart** took the first spacewalk in the new Apollo spacesuit. This had a portable life-support pack, which allowed an astronaut to explore unattached to the spacecraft.

Apollo 9 confirmed that all the systems worked in space as well as on the ground. The Moon was within reach. On Earth, anticipation grew.

APOLLO 10

Apollo 10 was to be a full dress rehearsal for the Moon landing. It would do everything except land on the Moon. In lunar orbit the Lunar Module separated from the Command Module, positioning the astronauts only 14 kilometres above the lunar surface.

Disaster almost struck while **Thomas Stafford** and **Eugene 'Gene' Cernan** orbited the Moon in the Lunar Module. It began to turn over and over, completely out of control. This continued for eight terrifying seconds before Stafford managed to stop the tumble.

When Apollo 10 splashed down safely on May 26, 1969, the stage was set for **Apollo 11** . . .

In July, 1969, time was running out to achieve the United States' goal of landing on the Moon by the end of the decade. The Apollo programme had recovered from its disastrous start and achieved everything it set out to do – except an actual Moon landing.

In June, 1969, United States spy satellites had seen a huge Soviet rocket being prepared for launch, followed in July by evidence that it had exploded on the launch pad. This was the N-1 (page 47). There would be two more failed N-1 test flights, and their failure ended Russia's manned Moon landing programme.

Meanwhile, Apollo 11 was ready to launch. The main objective of the mission – of course – was to land on the Moon and return safely, but while the astronauts were there, they were going to be busy. No one knew how easy it would be to move around and how well equipment would work on the lunar surface, so everything the crew did would be recorded and studied. They were also to collect data about the lunar surface, including rock samples and experiments to investigate cosmic rays, seismic activity and solar winds.

In the United States – and the rest of the world – excitement grew. By launch day, 16 July, around one million people had gathered near Cape Kennedy to watch Apollo 11 lift off.

APOLLO 11 - THE CREW

The first men to set foot on the Moon would instantly become world famous. You might assume that they were very carefully chosen by NASA with this in mind, but they weren't. **Deke Slayton**, former Mercury 7 astronaut and in 1969 NASA's Director of Flight Operations, was in charge of selecting the astronauts and he felt that any crew should be trained to fly any mission. The crew that would man Apollo 11 were:

APOLLO 11

NEIL ARMSTRONG
5/8/1930–25/8/2012
BIRTHPLACE: OHIO, UNITED STATES
FLYING EXPERIENCE: NAVAL PILOT IN THE KOREAN WAR WHERE HE WON THREE MEDALS; BECAME A TEST PILOT AFTER COMPLETING A DEGREE IN AERONAUTICAL ENGINEERING
SPACE MISSIONS: GEMINI 8 (1966); COMMANDER, APOLLO 11 (1969)
TOTAL TIME IN SPACE: 8 DAYS, 14 HOURS
Made his first flight in a plane when he was six and decided immediately that he wanted to be a pilot. He took lessons while still at school and made his first solo flight aged 16.

BUZZ ALDRIN (Born Edwin Eugene Aldrin Jr.)
20/1/1930
BIRTHPLACE: NEW JERSEY, UNITED STATES
FLYING EXPERIENCE: UNITED STATES AIR FORCE PILOT IN THE KOREAN WAR; AWARDED THE DISTINGUISHED FLYING CROSS
SPACE MISSIONS: GEMINI 12 (1966); LUNAR MODULE PILOT, APOLLO 11 (1969)
TOTAL TIME IN SPACE: 12 DAYS, 1 HOUR
Nicknamed 'Buzz' because as a child his sister kept pronouncing 'brother' as 'buzzer'. On the Gemini 12 mission he completed three space walks, spending a total of five and a half hours in the vacuum of space.

APOLLO 11

APOLLO 11

MICHAEL COLLINS
31/10/1930
BIRTHPLACE: ROME, ITALY (UNITED STATES ARMY BASE)
FLYING EXPERIENCE: UNITED STATES AIR FORCE PILOT; TEST PILOT AT EDWARDS AIRFORCE BASE, CALIFORNIA
SPACE MISSIONS: GEMINI 10 (1966); COMMAND MODULE PILOT, APOLLO 11 (1969)
TOTAL TIME IN SPACE: 11 DAYS, 2 HOURS
His first space flight was on Gemini 10. He designed the Apollo 11 mission patch, the embroidered design worn by crew on a space flight.

THE WORLD IS WATCHING

As Apollo 11 prepared to launch, streets were deserted in many countries, as families gathered in living rooms and almost everyone who *owned* a TV tuned in. Lift-off was watched by an estimated one billion people – the biggest TV audience up to then – at a time when far fewer households had a TV (and TVs had *much* smaller screens) than they do today.

In the ABC news studio, mock-ups of the Command Module and Lunar Module had been built to help viewers understand what was happening, and the ABC commentators at the launch site wore the same liquid-cooled underwear as the Apollo crew!

Walter Cronkite, the most famous news broadcaster in the United States, covered the launch for CBS News and would continue to report on the rest of the mission.

In under an hour and a half, Apollo 11 will lift off on the voyage man has always dreamed about – next stop, the Moon. Many things will never be the same again.

T minus 1 minute and counting. 40 seconds away from the Apollo 11 lift-off.

10...9...8...7...6... Ignition sequence starts... 5...4...3...2...1...0. All engines running. Lift-off. We have a lift-off. Oh boy, oh boy, it looks good. The building's shaking!

On 16 July, 1969, Apollo 11, crewed by Neil Armstrong, Buzz Aldrin and Michael Collins, lifted off from Kennedy Space Center. They orbited Earth one and a half times, then the engine of Saturn V's S-IVB third stage (page 50) fired to send them towards the Moon.

Three days later they entered lunar orbit and, 24 hours after that, the Lunar Module, *Eagle*, separated from the Command Module, *Columbia*. Michael Collins stayed in the Command Module, and Buzz Aldrin and Neil Armstrong started to descend to the Moon's surface.

After an hour, the engine fired to slow them for landing, but the Lunar Module overshot the landing zone. Armstrong switched to a semi-automatic landing mode, as the automatic programme was sending them to an area covered in boulders. It was a risky manoeuvre. A signal warning that there was only 60 seconds of fuel left sounded . . . Armstrong was able to land safely, just in time.

"Tranquility Base here. The Eagle has landed," said Neil Armstrong.
"Man on the Moon!" said Walter Cronkite. "Oh boy. Nothing compares with this."

Four hours later, after Armstrong and Aldrin had completed their checks, a blurry image of the Lunar Module appeared on TV screens.

"There's a foot coming down the steps," said Cronkite . . .

THE EAGLE HAS LANDED

After the Lunar Module, *Eagle,* touched down in an area of the Moon known as the Sea of Tranquility on 20 July, 1969, Neil Armstrong took the final step off the Lunar Module's ladder and onto the Moon's surface. It was then that he spoke the famous words, **"This is one small step for man, one giant leap for mankind."** Twenty minutes later, he was joined by Buzz Aldrin, for the first conversation on the Moon.

Isn't that something! Magnificent sight out here.

It was a tight squeeze to get out of the Lunar Module hatch. The bulky spacesuits and large life-support packs weren't easy to get through such a small opening.

Magnificent desolation.

The pair spent over two hours taking photos, collecting samples and setting up scientific equipment before returning to the Lunar Module to sleep. How could they shut their eyes knowing they were on the Moon?

WE CAME IN PEACE
FOR ALL MANKIND

LEAVING THE MOON Once they were both on the surface of the Moon, Armstrong and Aldrin planted a United States flag and began to take photographs. They had a short telephone conversation with President Nixon before starting to collect rock samples and setting up science experiments.

They had to work quickly, as they would only spend two and a half hours outside. The rest of the time was spent on vital but much less exciting tasks: checking systems, eating, resting and preparing for lift-off. Finally, 21 hours, 36 minutes after touching down, it was time to head home.

While preparing to take off, Armstrong or Aldrin brushed against a switch needed to fire the engine for lift-off . . . and broke it. Luckily, they were able to operate what was left of it with a pen!

WHAT THEY BROUGHT BACK FROM THE MOON

Over 20 kilograms of Moon rock samples. They left behind everything they didn't need, to make the *Eagle* as light as possible for lift-off.

WHAT THEY LEFT ON THE MOON

A plaque that read: **"Here men from the planet Earth first set foot upon the Moon, July 1969 AD. We came in peace for all mankind."**

A capsule containing goodwill messages from four United States presidents and 73 other world leaders.

A gold olive branch as a symbol of peace.

Medals awarded to Yuri Gagarin and Vladimir Komarov.

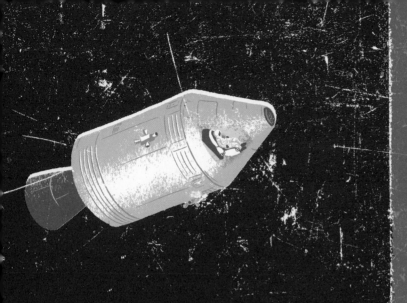

CALCULATE YOUR MOON WEIGHT!

Your weight depends on gravity. Because lunar gravity is only about one sixth of what it is on Earth, so is your weight. In theory, you could jump about 3 metres high and stay up for around 4 seconds on the Moon, but astronauts didn't get that high because their spacesuits were not flexible enough.

Earth Weight (kg)	Moon Weight (kg)
1	0.17
10	1.67
20	3.33
30	5.00
40	6.67
50	8.33
60	10.0
70	11.7
80	13.3
90	15.0

ALL ALONE IN THE NIGHT . . .

When the *Eagle* separated from *Columbia*, Michael Collins was left in orbit. He was out of communication with Earth for 48 minutes of each orbit, when the Command Module was behind the Moon, 250,000 miles from Earth.

"I am alone now, truly alone and absolutely isolated from any known life. I am it," he wrote as he orbited the Moon.

Science experiments. One of them, which measures the distance between Earth and the Moon, is still in use.

An Apollo 1 mission patch in memory of Chaffee, Grissom and White.

Backpacks

Boots

The most famous footprints in history.

Cameras

Containers for pee, poo and puke. The official list doesn't say if they were full or not . . .

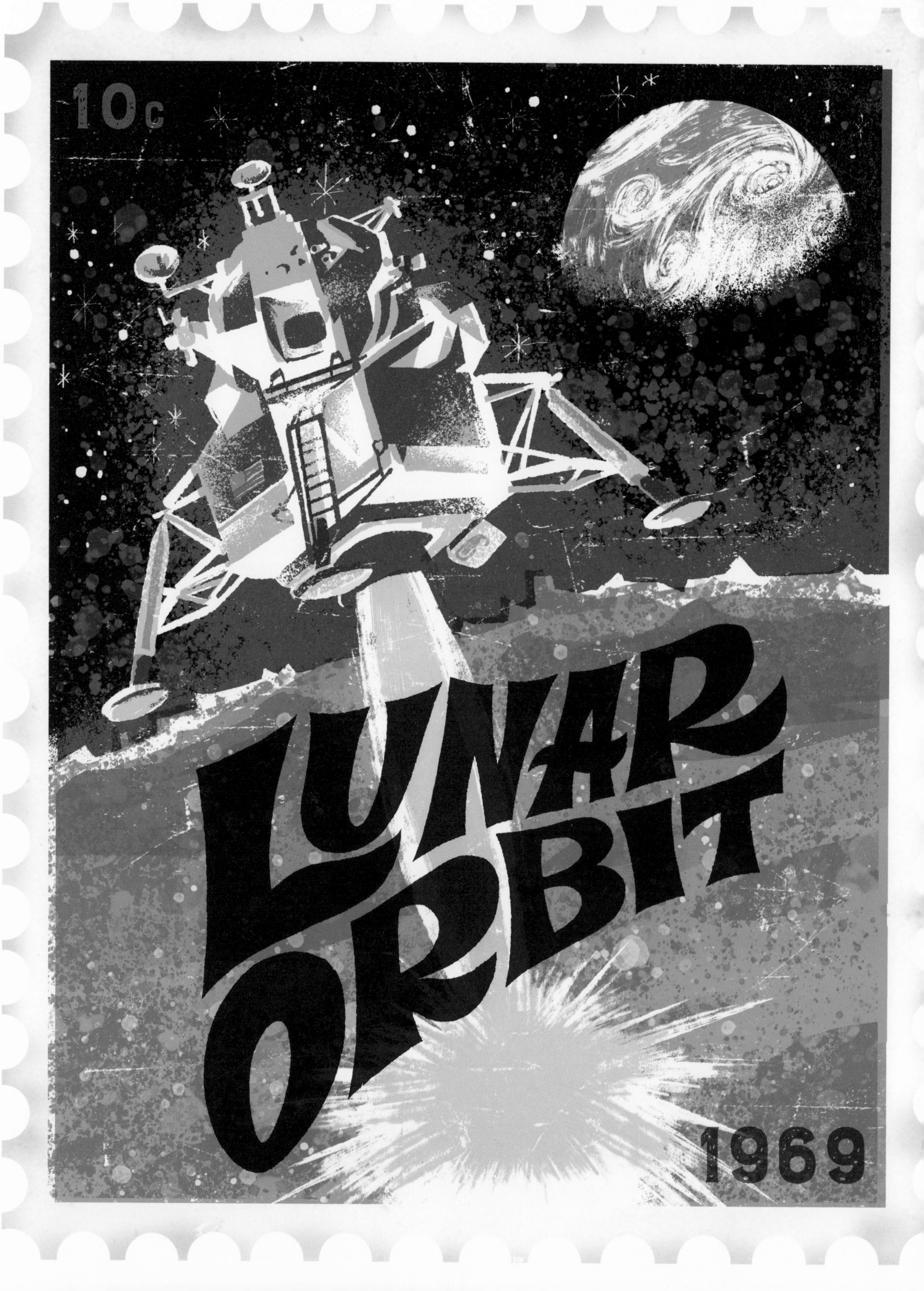
10c
LUNAR
ORBIT
1969

The race to put a human on the Moon was over, won by the United States. On greeting the Apollo 11 crew when they returned, President Nixon said, "This is the greatest week in the history of the world."

Congratulations poured in from many countries, including the Soviet Union, and commemorative magazine articles, stamps and special coins were produced. The Apollo 11 astronauts went on tour, and met many world leaders.

Now it was time to explore the Moon more fully. Apollo 12 – the second mission to the Moon – launched successfully, despite being struck by lightning as it lifted off, and landed in the south-eastern sector of the Moon known as the Ocean of Storms. Astronauts **Charles 'Pete' Conrad** and **Alan LaVern Bean** spent a total of 11 hours working on the Moon's surface, carrying out experiments and collecting samples. The Command Module pilot was **Richard Francis 'Dick' Gordon**. They should also have sent back high-quality colour TV footage, but unfortunately one of the astronauts accidentally pointed the camera at the sun, which broke it.

The aim of the Apollo missions went far beyond landing on the Moon. The United States wanted to show that it was the most successful nation in space. A vital part of this was to explore the Moon and assess people's ability to work there, as well as developing technology for other aspects of space exploration. Now Apollo 13, with its Command Module, *Odyssey*, and Lunar Module, *Aquarius*, was about to take off, ready to achieve some of these goals.

APOLLO 13: THE GREAT ESCAPE

3...2...1... lift-off!

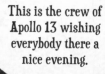

On 11 April, 1970, astronauts Jim Lovell, Jack Swigert, and Fred Haise boarded the *Odyssey* spacecraft. Their mission, Apollo 13, would be the third to land on the Moon.

At 46 hours and 43 minutes after lift-off, it looked like this would be the smoothest flight so far. At Mission Control:

The spacecraft is in real good shape . . . we're bored to tears down here.

And the world settled in to watch another successful mission to the Moon on TV.

This is the crew of Apollo 13 wishing everybody there a nice evening.

Nine minutes later, during a routine procedure . . .

HSSS! BANG!

One of the Service Module's two oxygen tanks had blown up.

In the Command Module:

Houston, we've had a problem here.

Even more concerning . . .

We are venting something out into space . . .

It's a gas of some sort!

The second oxygen tank was leaking.

If pressure drops below **100** the last fuel cell will die.

It's going down . . .

At Mission Control, it was soon clear there was only one way to get the astronauts home.

We are starting to think about using the Lunar Module as a lifeboat.

With 15 minutes of power left in the Service Module, the astronauts entered the Lunar Module to make the journey home. It was time to attempt something that had never been done before . . .

. . . using the Lunar Module, *Aquarius*, to steer the Command Module, *Odyssey*, back to Earth.

But the Lunar Module was not designed for re-entry, so on reaching Earth the astronauts had to return to the Command Module, which had the heat shields needed to protect them. They separated from *Aquarius* moments before re-entry. Would they make it home? Had the heat shields been damaged?

Farewell *Aquarius*, we salute you!

As the Command Module re-entered Earth's atmosphere, Mission Control lost contact.

Odyssey, Huston. Standing by. Over.

There was no way to know how the astronauts fared.

Odyssey, Huston . . .

Finally . . .

Hey, Joe.

They made it!

Five days, 22 hours, 54 minutes and 51 seconds since they had lifted off, the crew of Apollo 13 splashed down in the Pacific Ocean.

The return journey had been filled with anxiety and discomfort: the crew had limited heat and water, and poor visibility had made navigation difficult. Although Apollo 13 didn't land on the Moon, it was an incredible rescue mission. Despite the odds stacked against them, the crew returned to Earth unharmed.

APOLLO 14 TO 17

Nine months after the 'successful failure' of Apollo 13 and following enquiries and modifications, the Apollo Programme was ready to go again. But the end was in sight: the planned Apollo 18, 19 and 20 missions were all cancelled.

The objectives for **APOLLO 14,** which launched 31 January, 1971, were those Apollo 13 had not managed to achieve. Almost all of these were completed on the mission. Alan Shepard, first American in space, was Commander for this mission, and at 47 become the oldest man to walk on the Moon – and the only one to play golf while he was there. Mission Control tried to give him some tips . . .

You need to bend your knees a little more. Keep your head down.

I'm . . . wearing a space suit.

Just trying to help.

APOLLO 15, 16 AND 17, which took place between July, 1971, and December, 1972, went so well that Moon landings began to seem routine. They all used a **Lunar Roving Vehicle**, a four-wheeled buggy which allowed the astronauts to travel much further from their landing sites, and bring back more samples. These missions also spent far longer on the Moon, with the crew of Apollo 17 staying on the surface for 75 hours.

EUGENE CERNAN took the final step off the surface of the Moon. As the ascent stage of Apollo 17's Lunar Module lifted off, it left behind the descent stage, with a plaque that read, **"Here, man completed his first explorations of the Moon. December 1972 AD. May the spirit of peace in which he came be reflected in the lives of all mankind."**

When Apollo 17 splashed down near American Samoa on 19 December, 1972, the Moon landings were over.

The United States made six manned Moon landings between 1969 and 1972. The Apollo Programme confirmed that humans could work outside a spacecraft for extended periods, raising the possibility of long stays on space stations and manned missions to Mars.

In the fifty years since the first Moon landing, space stations like Skylab (United States, 1973–1979) and Mir (Russian, 1986–2001) have allowed research projects to take place in orbit, and the International Space Station (ISS) has provided opportunities for many different countries to collaborate. Today many astronauts come from different ethnicities and men and women from 37 countries have gone into space.

It took 19 years after Valentina Tereshkova's mission for a second woman to go to space. This was Russian cosmonaut **Svetlana Savitskaya** in 1982. From the 1980s, more women became astronauts – including **Helen Sharman**, who became the UK's first astronaut in 1991, and **Mae Carol Jemison** who became the first African American woman astronaut in 1992.

Robotic probes have reached every planet in the solar system and Mars has been surveyed in detail. Most recently, NASA's New Horizons probe has sent back pictures of the dwarf planet Ultima Thule, the most distant object in the Solar System to be explored. In January 2019, the Chinese robotic probe Chang'e-4 made the first ever landing on the far side of the Moon.

WHAT WE DISCOVERED

The Apollo flights gave us lots of new information about the Moon. Since then, there have been many robotic missions from which we have learned even more. We now know a great deal about the structure of the Moon and its violent past. It has been shaped by volcanic eruptions, asteroid impacts and meteorite strikes.

SEA OF TRANQUILITY

Three new chemical elements were discovered here: **Armalcolite**, (named for Armstrong, Aldrin and Collins); **Tranquillityte**; and **Pyroxferroite**. They are now known to exist on Earth too.

OCEAN OF STORMS

This enormous **'lunar mare'** (a low, flat plane on the Moon's surface) was created by lava flow from ancient volcanoes.

COPERNICUS AND TYCHO CRATERS

Formed by **meteor impacts**. Analysis of material from the craters has helped scientists work out when this happened.

APOLLO LANDING SITES

Moon rock samples from here confirm that Earth and the Moon contain the same minerals.

THE AGE OF PLANETS

The study of rock samples and craters has helped scientists work out how old **Earth, Mercury, Venus** and **Mars** must be.

To many people's disappointment, there is absolutely no sign of life on the Moon, and no sign that there ever has been any.

WHAT HAS SPACE TRAVEL DONE FOR LIFE ON EARTH?

You may think that space travel doesn't affect your life, but you're wrong. You've probably worn or used space technology today. In a way, we're all earthbound astronauts . . .

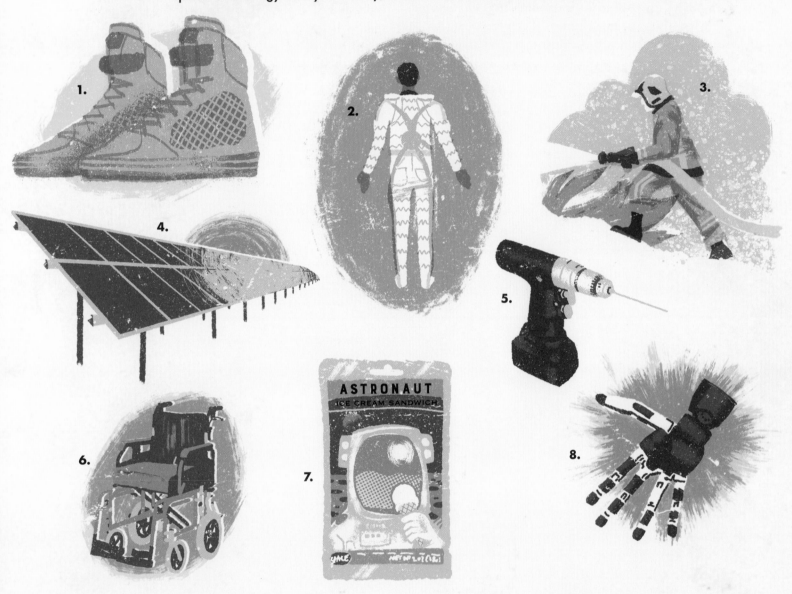

1. The construction of **moonboots** has led to the use of new materials in trainer insoles.

2. NASA's **Cool Suit technology** is now used for racing drivers' suits and in clothes for people born with no sweat glands.

3. Cool Suit and **flameproof fabrics** developed for spacesuits are now found in clothes and breathing systems for firefighters.

4. Solar panels are now widely used to generate electricity and smaller solar cells can power devices like calculators.

5. Cordless power tools, vacuum cleaners and surgical instruments are now commonplace. They were developed so astronauts could use them outside their modules.

6. Memory foam was developed by NASA to keep test pilots and astronauts properly cushioned during flights. It's now used in everything from mattresses to prosthetic limbs and wheelchair cushions.

7. Freeze-dried food was developed to reduce the weight of food carried during space flights.

8. NASA's work on robotics and artificial muscle systems has also led to **prosthetic limbs** with much better movement.

THE FUTURE

How far will humans travel in space? Although astronauts haven't gone beyond Earth orbit since 1972, we have expanded the distances robotic craft have travelled in space. The probes Voyager 1 and 2, launched in 1977, have left the Solar System, and Voyager 1 is now over 18 billion kilometres from Earth – the furthest anything built by humans has travelled. Several countries have plans to land probes on Mars in the 2020s. Making it possible for astronauts to travel further is more difficult, but NASA is currently working on an orbiting lunar platform. This would allow humans to go further into the Solar System than ever before.

WILL HUMANS LEAVE THE SOLAR SYSTEM?

The **Breakthrough Starshot Programme** plans to launch hundreds of phone-sized robot StarChip craft to survey the planet Proxima Centauri b, which is part of the nearest star system. It would take the craft 20 years to get there and four years to send data back to Earth. That might sound like a long time, but it would take thousands of years to get there at the speed of the fastest spacecraft now operating.

Maybe one day, the information we learn from the programme will lead to humans walking on a planet in another solar system.

WILL HUMANS WALK ON MARS?

There are tentative plans to send humans to Mars in the 2030s, but huge challenges need to be overcome for this to happen. Much of the technology needed to get to Mars already exists, but the journey would take several months, and the big problem with that is how such a long time in space would affect astronauts, both physically and mentally.

Researchers are working to develop **laser or nuclear powered spacecraft**. If these work, they could cut the journey time to around 45 days – but it will be many years before these new methods can be used to send a crew to Mars.

WILL I GO TO SPACE ON HOLIDAY?

You may not want to work in space, but what are the chances you will be able to go there on holiday? Some paying passengers have already travelled on Mir and the ISS, but they helped with research, so weren't simply tourists. Several companies are developing ideas for space tourism, however, and one of them even has plans for a **luxury orbiting hotel.** Perhaps you should start saving for that trip now . . .

HOW DO I BECOME AN ASTRONAUT?

You'll have to be determined and hard working – and patient. Study science, maths or engineering to degree level. You'll also need to qualify as an aircraft pilot if you want to pilot a spacecraft. You need to be adaptable and good at solving problems – and make sure you keep fit.

If you are a United States citizen, you can apply to NASA. If not, you can apply through one of the other space agencies. The odds of being selected are very small, but don't worry – there are lots of other space-related jobs here on Earth.

SPACE CAREERS ON EARTH

Here on Earth you could be an **astrophysicist** studying the planets and stars, or a **biologist** finding ways to stop astronauts' muscles wasting during space voyages. You could be an **astrobotanist** testing plants to see which ones can be grown on the Moon, or an **engineer, chemist, designer, lawyer, doctor** or **psychologist** specialising in space – there will be dozens of space-related careers.

If that space hotel gets built, it won't just be astronauts going into space. The hotel will need lots of staff – chefs and cleaners, bar staff and entertainers – just imagine what a dancer could do in low gravity!

And as time goes on, there will be jobs we can't even imagine now. The sky's not the limit for humans any more: we've got a whole universe to explore.